Humans Aren't Real!

'Humans Aren't Real!'
An original concept by Lou Treleaven
© Lou Treleaven 2022

Illustrated by Marina Halak

Published by MAVERICK ARTS PUBLISHING LTD

Studio 11, City Business Centre, 6 Brighton Road,
Horsham, West Sussex, RH13 5BB
© Maverick Arts Publishing Limited February 2022
+44 (0)1403 256941

A CIP catalogue record for this book is available at the British Library.

ISBN 978-1-84886-859-5

Maverick
publishing

www.maverickbooks.co.uk

Gold

This book is rated as: Gold Band (Guided Reading)

Humans Aren't Real!

by Lou Treleaven

illustrated by Marina Halak

Chapter 1

No one on Planet Blobb thought humans existed. Well, no one except Zarkle. She was sure they did. After all, Planet Blobb couldn't be the only planet in the universe with life, could it?

Zarkle loved reading stories about humans. She loved the stories so much she would read three at once, one with each eye. The stories were called things like *The Day the*

Humans Came and *Planet of the Humans*. No one seemed to know what a human might look like. Zarkle thought they might have two arms and maybe two eyes. That would be very strange.

If only she could meet a real human and find out!

Sometimes Zarkle just couldn't stop talking about humans. Her dad didn't mind, but her little brother made fun of her.

"You're silly! Humans aren't real!" Flon laughed.

"But you believe in Blobberfairies, Flon," said Zarkle. "If you can believe in those, surely I can believe in humans!"

On World Dream Day, the children all went to school dressed up as something from their dreams.

Zarkle made some hair out of strands of poppleweed. She drew hands and feet and stuck them on her tentacles. Then she covered up one of her eyes. She looked just like a human from her dreams!

It was fun seeing the other children's costumes.

"I'm Superblobber!" shouted Pryax.

"I'm a blobbercorn!" said Smig.

"I play floaty ball for Blobbers United!" lots of the children yelled.

Zarkle was the only one dressed as a human. At least, she thought she was...

Suddenly a strange upright creature with two legs walked towards her across the playground. Zarkle's tentacles shook with excitement. A real human!

"I come in peace. Take me to your leader!" said a funny voice.

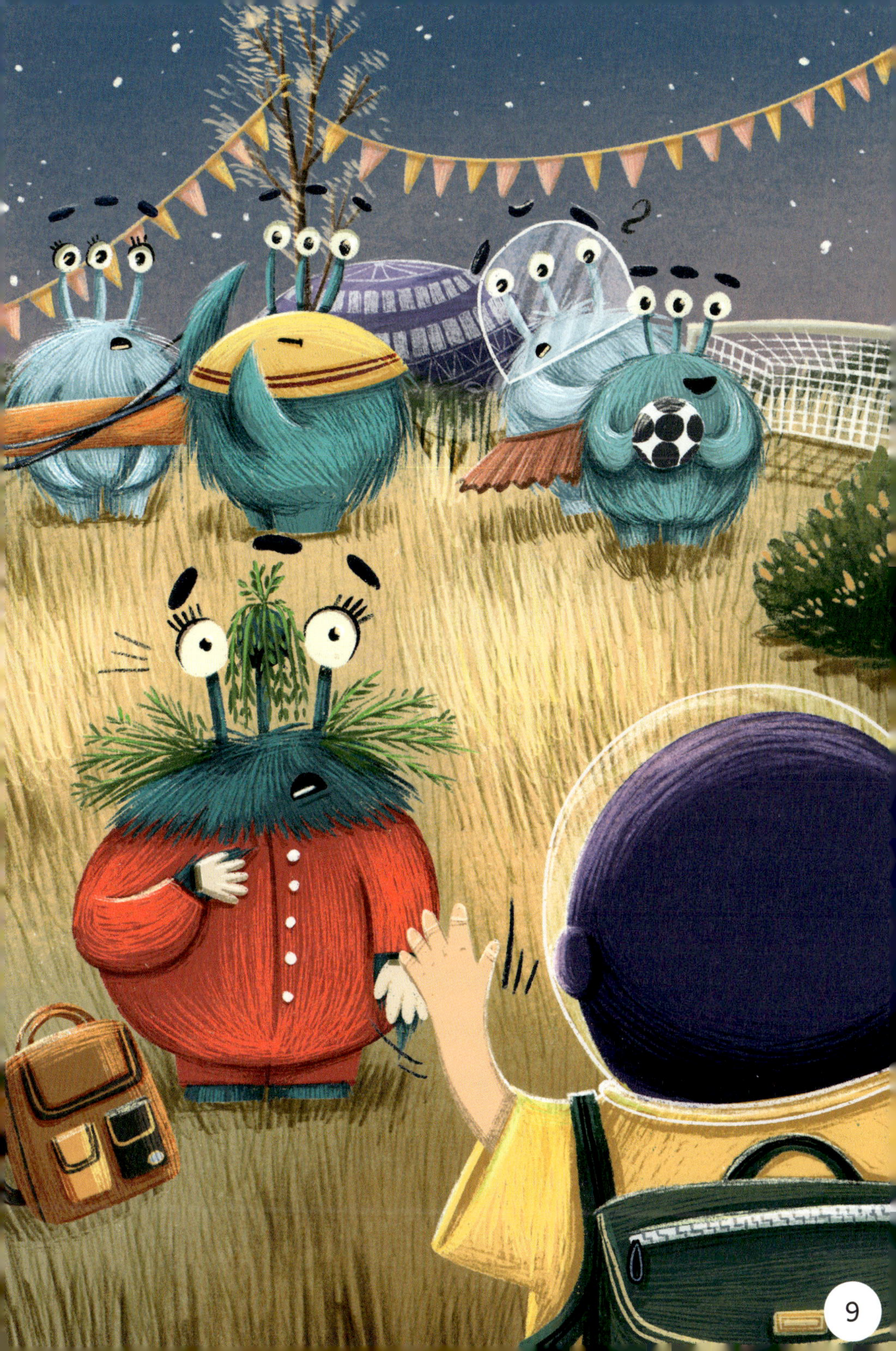

Chapter 2

Zarkle could see it wasn't a real human now, but it was a good costume.

"Hello, I'm Noop. I'm new. I'm new Noop," said Noop, taking off his mask.

"I'm Zarkle," Zarkle said happily. Someone else who liked humans! From that moment on, Zarkle and Noop were best friends.

Mrs Fizzle said they could choose a science project to work on in pairs. Zarkle and Noop knew exactly what subject to choose – humans!

"You can't do a science project about humans," said Pryax. "Humans aren't real!"

To Zarkle's surprise, Mrs Fizzle disagreed. "Why don't you use your project to show us that humans might be real?" she suggested. Zarkle and Noop looked at each other.

This project was going to be fun!

Zarkle invited Noop to her house after school. They read lots of stories about humans. They watched Zarkle's favourite bubble video, *The Human Spotters*!
But all the stories and videos were made up. No one had ever seen a real human. No one even knew where they lived.

"Maybe humans will come and find us one day?" Noop suggested.

"I don't know," said Zarkle. Her tentacles drooped. "Maybe Flon and Pryax are right. Humans aren't real…"

Chapter 3

When Noop's mother came to pick him up in her hover car, it was dark. Up above them, the stars twinkled. The more they looked, the more stars they could see. Stars upon stars upon stars.

"I wonder how many there are?" Zarkle said.

"Scientists think there are a billion stars just in our galaxy," said Noop's mother.

"And there are billions of galaxies out there with billions and billions of planets!"

Zarkle thought about this. "Do you think some of those planets might have humans on them?" she asked.

"Well, yes," said Noop's mother. "I suppose they might."

16

Soon it was time for Zarkle and Noop to show the class their project. They dressed up as humans again. First they showed the class a picture of the planet Blobb. Then they showed a picture of the system Blobb was a part of. Planet Blobb and three other planets went around a sun called Spark.

"But Spark isn't the only sun," explained Zarkle. "There are billions of galaxies, and billions and billions of planets!"

"So even if we've never seen a human, they probably exist," said Noop. "With so many planets out there, it would be weird if they didn't."

"Unfortunately humans may be too far away to find us," Zarkle said. "And we're too far away to find them. But they are out there, somewhere. Maybe a human is thinking about us right now. Maybe they are wondering if we are real!"

Everybody laughed. It was funny to think of someone not believing in them.

"Well done," said Mrs Fizzle. "I think you've convinced everyone that humans could exist."

"Hurray!" said Noop. "Does that mean we can come to school dressed as humans every day?"

"Not every day," said Mrs Fizzle, smiling. Zarkle was quiet. For some reason she felt sad.

Chapter 4

"How did the presentation go?" asked Zarkle's dad when he got back from work at the hover car factory.

"Brilliant," Zarkle said flatly. "But now I know – I'm never going to see a human. They're too far away. It would take years and years for them to get here."

Dad hugged her. "Don't give up hope. Here, maybe this will help."

He gave her a present. Zarkle unwrapped it. It was a telescope! "Wow! Thanks, Dad!"

Zarkle looked up at the sky every night through her new telescope. Stars upon stars upon stars.

Which star belonged to the humans? She wished she knew.

One night she saw an odd shape shoot past. She chased it with her telescope. It looked like a plate or dish on its side with bits stuck on the bottom, and it was moving fast. It didn't look like a spaceship. But it did look like something made to travel through space for a long time.

25

Maybe it was sent by humans!

"Dad! Dad!" Zarkle called.

"Ssh, you'll wake up Flon," Dad said, coming in. "What is it?"

"There's something in the sky! Look!"

Dad looked through the telescope. "So there is! There's some strange symbols on it."

"Strange human symbols!" Zarkle cried. "I knew it, humans are real!" She waved her tentacles happily.

"I think you might be right, Zarkle!" Dad agreed.

Chapter 5

A long way away across the stars, on Planet Earth, two humans called Lucy and Greg were doing a presentation to their class about aliens. Greg held up a picture of Voyager 1.

"Scientists sent this space probe out a long time ago," Lucy said. "It's now gone further than anything else we have sent into space, and it's still going."

29

"Scientists put a Golden Record inside Voyager 1. This is a special disc with sounds and pictures from Earth. So if aliens ever find Voyager 1, they'll be able to learn all about us," said Greg. "I wonder if they've found it yet?"

The End

Book Bands for Guided Reading

The Institute of Education book banding system is a scale of colours that reflects the various levels of reading difficulty. The bands are assigned by taking into account the content, the language style, the layout and phonics. Word, phrase and sentence level work is also taken into consideration.

Maverick Early Readers are a bright, attractive range of books covering the pink to white bands. All of these books have been book banded for guided reading to the industry standard and edited by a leading educational consultant.

To view the whole Maverick Readers scheme, visit our website at www.maverickearlyreaders.com

Or scan the QR code above to view our scheme instantly!